The
Lurking
Chronology

A Timeline of the Derleth Mythos

By Pete Rawlik

Lovecraft ezine press

www.LovecraftZine.com

Copyright Pete Rawlik 2015

Cover Art by Steve Santiago

Published by Lovecraft eZine Press

Formatting by Kenneth W. Cain

1. Introduction

When I write stories set in the Greater Miskatonic Milieu I rely heavily on Peter Cannon's excellent study of Lovecraft's works *The Chronology Out of Time*. It is a masterpiece of research that deserves greater recognition as perhaps the definitive work of its sort. Its very existence spurred me on to create my own tales by identifying several key events throughout Lovecraft's fictional history, without it *Reanimators* wouldn't exist.

That said I've always been disappointed that Cannon didn't include Derleth's posthumous collaborations, I understand the logic, I just wish they had been included. So years ago I began taking notes, and building on Cannon's original adding in Derleth and Lin Carter and any other mythos dates I could find. Some of this went into creating a piece of pseudo-history concerning Miskatonic Valley, but that project ground to a halt after all these notes revealed a fascinating little tidbit that drove me to write a novel, which in turn inspired *Reanimators*. But I still had thousands of notes on hundreds of stories; they were just sitting there begging to be used. I know exactly what motivated me to transform my notes on the stories of August Derleth into the volume you now hold, but decency prevents me from explaining it here. Regardless, some time ago I plunged into organizing my notes and getting them collated for publication.

It hasn't been easy. The decisions I made years ago for my own purposes, I now have to justify to the world.

First off, I have to acknowledge the use of Chris Jarocha-Ernst's excellent bibliography which provided a specific list of Cthulhu Mythos stories written by Derleth, as well as the posthumous

Lovecraft collaborations. I have also chosen to include those stories that Derleth co-authored with others. Excluded is the unfinished "Watchers Out of Time", and "The Lamp of Alhazred", which in my opinion is meta-fictional in nature, as well as all of the Solar Pons stories and novels, which if included would have overshadowed the other stories by sheer volume.

As noted by Cannon in preparing the Lovecraft chronology, many stories contain evidence to establish a month or a particular day, but not a year. When possible, I have reviewed internal evidence and made decisions based on context clues, and detailed my logic with explanatory notes. In some cases no data at all exists and the action must be set at an arbitrary date which I note. In cases where dates are vague I have used the term circa.

I must acknowledge the work of fellow scholar Rick Lai in the preparation of this document. In his article "The Distortion Over Innsmouth" he notes that when it comes to the events in Innsmouth Derleth tends to contradict Lovecraft, particularly with the date of the Federal occupation. Likewise, Lai, and Robert Price have both noted the confusion generated by Derleth's character Obadiah Marsh, and Lovecraft's Obed Marsh. While many suggest that Obadiah be treated as an ancestor of Obed, Lai suggests that Derleth was treating The "Shadow Out of Innsmouth" as a fictionalized version of actual events, in other words Lovecraft's tale of Obed was an obfuscation of events involving Obadiah. This idea is consistent with Derleth's inclusion of Lovecraft as a character (albeit deceased) and the periodic usage of *The Outsider and Others* as a source of mythos knowledge. While I find Derleth's act of fictionalizing "The Shadow Out of Innsmouth" unpalatable, I must admit that Lai's proposal is an attractive explanation to some interesting contextual problems.

The Lai proposal explains several stories that are central to the Derleth Mythos. "The Shuttered Room", which is a blend of themes from "The Shadow Over Innsmouth" and "The Dunwich Horror" suddenly makes more sense if the decay of Innsmouth is slowed and the Federal occupation is stretched into a building action as opposed to a sudden invasion. Similarly the visit of Dr. Charriere to Arkham/Innsmouth in the mid-19th Century to look at supposed Deep Ones makes more sense if the transformation is not just genetic but also infectious as hinted at by Derleth. This idea that the metamorphosis can be initiated by simple association rather than genetics is also suggested by events in "The Fisherman of Falcon Point" and by "Innsmouth Clay".

"Innsmouth Clay" poses an additional chronological problem. The text of this story sets the time of action in 1927 -1928, however the description of Innsmouth is of a post Federal assault which Derleth in "The Black Island" has beginning in the spring of 1928, and culminating that summer. Since "The Black Island" was written twenty years earlier than "Innsmouth Clay" I have chosen to use the earlier story as the standard, and modified the events in the later story by one year.

It must be noted that this bit of pseudo-scholarship is open for improvement. If you find errors or can suggest reasonable alternatives to the dates proposed here, and can provide supporting evidence, the chronology can be modified.

2. Key and Story Notes

Key to Stories	
BI The Black Island	PH The Peabody Heritage
BT Beyond the Threshold	RH The Return of Hastur
DB The Dark Brotherhood (1)	SA The Shadow in the Attic
DD The Dweller in Darkness	SC The Sandwin Compact
The	SM The Spawn of the Maelstrom (9)
GB The God Box (15)	SO The Seal of R'Lyeh
GS The Gorge Beyond Salapunco (3)	SR The Shuttered Room (10)
GW The Gable Window	SS The Shadow Out of Space
HC House on Curwen Street	ST Something from Out There (14)
HD The Horror From the Depths	SU The Survivor
HM Horror from the	SW Something in Wood

Middle Span		(11)	
HO The House in the Oaks (4)		TA The Ancestor (12)	
HV The House in the Valley (5)		TS Those Who Seek (13)	
IC Innsmouth Clay (16)		TW The Thing That Walked on the Winds	
IT Ithaqua (6)		WD Wentworth's Day	
KK The Keeper of the Key		WH Witches Hollow	
LS The Lair of the Star-Spawn (7)		WP The Whippoorwills in the Hills	
LT The Lurker at the Threshold (8)		WS The Watcher From the Sky	
PE The Passing of Eric Holm			

Explanatory Notes

1.   "The Dark Brotherhood" (1966) gives no year for the occurrence of events, but it makes mention of a Welsbach gas-lamp which were popular in the early Twentieth Century. Also mentioned is the fact that men were listening for radio signals from other planets. This might be a reference to Ohio State University's Big Ear, a radio telescope designed to search for extraterrestrial life which was completed in 1963. I have set the story in 1965.

2.   "The Fisherman of Falcon Point" clearly takes place prior to the fall of Innsmouth, before the full dominance of the Marsh Family, but after initial contact with the Deep Ones, the 1839 and 1842 dates are as good as any.

3.   There are no dates in "The Gorge Beyond Salapunco" to place either the current events or those of the *HMS Advocate* in the timeline. However, the complete lack of any references to World War II suggests that these things occurred prior to 1941. I have placed Boyd's actions in 1940 and the *Advocate* in 1937.

4.   "The House in the Oaks" Howard states that Justin Geoffrey died at 21. Lovecraft's "The Thing on the Doorstep" states that he died in 1926. Harms' *Encyclopedia Cthulhiana* states that Geoffrey was born in 1898 and died in 1926, which would have made him 27 or 28. Rick Lai suggests that after Howard abandoned "The House in the Oaks" fragment he revised his thinking on Geoffrey's age at death. It might be best to take 21 as a misread or misremembered 27.

5.   There are few clues in "The House in the Valley" to give the action a date. There is a mention of Rick's Lake which is likely a reference to "The Dweller in Darkness", and a recent hex murder which may refer to the murder of Alvin Faust of Berks County Pennsylvania in March 1940. I have placed the story in 1941.

6.   The timeline for the ending of "Ithaqua" is not well established, but I have assumed Dalhousie's leave from headquarters was about one month.

7.   There are no dates in "The Lair of the Star Spawn" (1932). However the opening suggests the action occurred almost 30 years ago. Rick Lai, in his essay *Fu-Manchu vs. Cthulhu* sets Fo-Lan's death in 1899 and the action in 1902. I see no reason to contradict this, though Beijing was not referred to as Peiping until June 1928, but this could be considered a later editorial change.

8.   "The Lurker at The Threshold" establishes several dates throughout the document which provide a timeline of events. However, readers might notice that between the times Ambrose Dewart arrives and when Stephen Bates begins investigating more than two years have passed though this is not apparent in the action.

9.   "The Spawn of the Maelstrom" (1939) has no dates; I have set the action in 1936.

10.   "The Shuttered Room" (1959) contains no dates. However there is a mention of Walt Whitman's new book which I suspect is a reference to *Democratic Vistas* of 1871. Additionally, the Innsmouth that Sarey visits seems not too decayed, and well before the Federal raid. Finally, Sarey visits Ralsa Marsh Obed's great-

grandson, which if we assume a generation passes every twenty years would add about sixty years since the birth of Obed's son, though this is not dated either. Given this data I set Sarey's visit to Innsmouth and her imprisonment in 1906. The later action is more difficult to place as Abner Whateley has been gone so long from Dunwich that he has lost count. However, the proprietor of the general store is Tobias Whateley who also appears in "The Horror From the Middle Span" which I set in 1949, and where he is described as old, which he is not in "The Shuttered Room". In order to shave some years off Tobias I have set Abner's return in 1934.

11.   There are no dates in "Something in Wood" (1948), however Derleth mentions artists Epstein and Mestrovic who were prominent in the late 1940s. I have placed the story in 1947.

12.   "The Ancestor", written in 1957 makes reference to an electric phonograph, the first all-transistor phonographs were marketed in the fall of 1955. I have therefore placed the events of this story in 1956.

13.   There are no dates in 1932's "Those Who Seek"; I have set the main action in 1929.

14.   There are no dates in "Something From Out There" from 1951. I have set it in 1950.

15.   The lack of references to the war in "The God Box" suggests that this London based story is set prior to 1939; I have set it in 1938.

The dates of this story sets the time of action in 1927 -1928, however the description of Innsmouth is of a post-Federal assault which Derleth in "The Black Island" has beginning in the Spring of 1928, and culminating that Summer. Since "The Black Island" was written twenty years earlier than "Innsmouth Clay" I have chosen to use the earlier story as the standard, and modified the events in "Innsmouth Clay" by one year.

3. A Chronology of August Derleth's Cthulhu Mythos Stories

447

The Saxons seize a stone temple from the Celts. (TS)

777

A party of Danes besieges an abbey near Manchester. (TS)

1537

Royal mercenaries raid an abandoned abbey. (TS)

1621-57

Sometime in this period the Wampanaug wonderworker Misquamacus tells Governor Bradford of the disappearance of Richard Billington. (LT)

1636

Jean-Francois Charriere is born in Bayonne, France. (SU)

1653-1656

Jean-Francois Charriere studies in Paris under the Royalist Richard Wiseman. (SU)

1600

Mid-century

Fr. Piregard disappears in the area that will one day be known as Pashepaho Wisconsin. (DD)

1674

Dr. Jean-Francois Charriere serves in the French Army in India. (SU)

1690

The Geoffrey Family settles in New York State. (HO)

1691

Earliest documentation of Dr. Jean-Francois Charriere living in Quebec. (SU)

1692

A Peabody is amongst those charged in Salem. (PH)

1697

Dr. Jean-Francois Charriere leaves Quebec for unknown parts. The Charriere House is built on Benefit Street in Providence. (SU)

1787

Jedediah Peabody moves from Salem to Wilbraham, Massachusetts where he builds a substantial estate. (PH)

1788

June 5

The High Sheriff burns the widow of John Doten and the child she
gave birth to the previous year, which is neither man nor beast but
the face of which bears a frightful resemblance to the long dead
Richard Billington. (LT)

1797

Laban Billington is born to Alijah Phineas Billington and his wife
Lavinia, but his mother does not live for long after the birth. (LT)

August

Captain Obadiah Marsh and First Mate Cyrus Alcott Phillips return
to Innsmouth harbor in a rowboat and report that their ship the Cory
was lost with all hands while in the Marquesas. Insinuations that
Obadiah and three others have wives in Ponape begin. (SO)

1801

A Boston publisher releases a new edition of the Reverend Ward
Phillips' *Thaumaturgical Prodigies in the New-English Canaan*. (LT)

1807

Over the course of the year at least six people vanish from the
Dunwich area including Wilbur Corey and Jedediah Tyndal both of
whom are found months later, after which Jonathan Bishop becomes
the last to disappear. (LT)

1808

A review by John Druven of Reverend Ward Phillips' book *Thaumaturgical Prodigies in the New-English Canaan*, incites a letter war between Phillips, Druven and Alijah Phineas Billington. Anonymous complaints about occurrences on Billington's property result in Phillips, Druven and Deliverance Westripp visiting Billington, after which Druven vanishes. Six months later Druven's body is found at the mouth of the Manuxet River. Soon after Alijiah Billington and his son Laban depart for England. (LT)

1839

Fisherman Enoch Conger catches and releases a "mermaid" off of Devil Reef. (FF)

1842

Fisherman Enoch Conger is injured at sea and returned home by fellow fisherman, that same day Doctor Gilman finds his home abandoned. Later that year Jedediah Harper and his crew see something strange in the water, after which the families of Marsh and Martin make sure the men never have to go out to sea again. (FF)

1846

Rumors about Obed Marsh bringing a plague to Innsmouth begin. (WS)

1850 circa

The Marsh Family led by Captain Obed Marsh has three ships: The brig Columbia, brig Hetty, and barque Sumatra Queen. (IC)

Leander Alwyn leaves Innsmouth and builds a house near Harmon Wisconsin. (BT)

Big Bob Hiller's lumber operation encroaches on the area surrounding Rick's Lake. Eighteen men are lost before Hiller pulls out of the area. (DD)

1851

Dr. Jean-Francois Charriere visits Asaph Goade in Arkham noting his batrachian appearance. (SU)

1857

Dr. Jean-Francois Charriere visits Harry Bishop in St. Augustine, Florida. (SU)

1861

Dr. Jean-Francois Charriere visits the Balzac Family in Charleston. (SU)

1863

Dr. Jean-Francois Charriere visits Innsmouth. (SU)

1869

Leander Alwyn leaves instructions concerning his property in the event of his death. (BT)

1871

Dr. Jean-Francois Charriere visits Jed Price "The Alligator Man". (SU)

1878

About this time near Old Dutch Town the feud between the Alders and the Abners concerning who owns the abandoned farmhouse that borders both their properties begins, with each side claiming the other is the property owner. (HO)

1899

Dr. Fo-Lan of Peiping is reportedly murdered. (LS)

1902

An unnamed great-grandson of Asaph Peabody is born (PH)

Three months out of New York the Hawks Expedition to Burma, led by Geoffrey Hawks, is attacked and killed by bandits. A month later student Eric Marsh is found alive. Not long after a Tokyo newspaper reports that Dr. Fo-Lan is alive. (LS)

1905

Many children go missing in the area surrounding Wilbraham, Massachusetts. Children report seeing a large black creature, while others are mauled or bitten. (PH)

1906

After visiting Innsmouth Sarah Whateley is imprisoned by her father Luther in the mill. (SR)

1907

Gamwell last sees Dr. Jean-Francois Charriere whom he guesses is at least 80 years old. (SU)

Asaph Peabody dies at the family estate, afterwards it is reported that Balor, his black cat, has not been seen since. (PH)

Over the course of a month a total of seventeen cattle and six sheep are killed in Dunwich. Later Ada Wilkerson and Howard Willie are killed as well. The shuttering of the Whateley Mill seems to bring an end to things. (SR)

1908

Late Summer

Justin Geoffrey, age 10, is lost overnight near Old Dutch Town. He is found sleeping peacefully in a grove of trees next to an abandoned farmhouse and speaks of extraordinary dreams. From this point on he is tortured by wild nightmares and insomnia. (HO)

1908-1914

Sometime during this period an unnamed grandson of Asaph Peabody dies. (PH)

1913

Probably year for the completion of Pr. Shrewsbury's *An Investigation into the Myth-Patterns of latter day Primitives with Especial Reference to the*

R'lyeh Text. (This date derives from Lin Carter's "Horror in the Gallery" AKA "Zoth-Ommog". This is necessary because although Derleth doesn't have the book published until 1936, it appears in Dr. Seneca Lapham's office in *The Lurker at the Threshold*, which is clearly set in 1924. Dan Harms suggests that the 1936 edition is a reprint, but I offer a simpler explanation: The book was not published until 1936 but existed as a manuscript, and possibly photostats of the manuscript until then).

1914–1918

Ambrose Dewart loses his son in the Great War. (LT)

1915

Wilbur Akeley graduates from Miskatonic University with a   degree in Archeology and then travels to Central Asia for three years of study. (GW)

May 7

An unnamed grandson of Asaph Peabody dies on the Lusitania. (PH)

September

Pr. Laban Shrewsbury leaves Arkham without notifying anyone. (HC)

1917

An unnamed grandson of Asaph Peabody dies on the Western Front. (PH)

1919

Wilbur Akeley begins three years of work in Central and South America. (GW)

1919

The son of Asaph Peabody dies, and the Peabody Estate is inherited by the sole surviving grandson. The property is looked after by the lawyer Ahab Hopkins who occasionally leases it out, but not for any length of time. (PH)

Seth Bishop begins visiting the Miskatonic University Library and copying passages from various occult volumes. The practice lasts until 1923. (HV)

1920

September

Mr. Williams of Brattleboro Vermont takes a teaching job at District School #7 about seven miles west of Arkham. (WH)

October

Six cows and a shed are crushed on the Dunlock Farm west of Arkham. A few days later Pr. Martin Keane and a schoolteacher named Williams are present when the farm belonging to the Potter Family burns. (WH)

1921

The Providence law firm of Baker and Greenbaugh is hired by Dr. Jean-Francois Charriere, though they never meet their client. (SU)

Wilbur Akeley is offered a position at Miskatonic University but instead buys and remodels the Old Wharton Place off Aylesbury Pike. (GW)

March

Ambrose Dewart of England, the great grandson of Laban Billington, comes to the Arkham area to inspect his family estate. (LT)

April

Ambrose Dewart advertises for assistance in restoring the Billington House off Aylesbury Pike. The restoration takes several months. (LT)

Summer

Ambrose Dewart moves in to the newly restored Billington House. (LT)

1922

Stephen Bates meets Dr. Armitage Harper of Miskatonic University at a conference in Boston. (LT)

Summer

North of Dunwich, Nahum Wentworth lends Amos Stark $5,000. (WD)

Fall

Amos Stark names Genie Wentworth as his sole heir after accidentally killing her father Nahum. (WD)

1923

Circa

In semi-retirement Dr. Nathaniel Corey moves from Boston to Arkham and opens up a practice. (SS)

October

Jason Osborn of Dunwich vanishes. Stephen Bates of Boston goes to visit his cousin Ambrose Dewart at Billington House and at the advice of Dr. Armitage Harper takes him to Boston for the winter. (LT)

December

Between Christmas and New Year's the body of a missing man is found in Dunwich the appearance of which suggests that it has fallen from a great height. (LT)

1924

February 2

The body of Jason Osborn is found in Dunwich the appearance of which suggests that it has fallen from a great height. (LT)

March

Wilbur Akeley dies of natural causes. His will creates the Akeley Collection of papers and rare books at Miskatonic University. His house near Dunwich is left to his cousin Fred Akeley. (GW)

Late March

Ambrose Dewart and his cousin Stephen Bates return to Billington House, within days Dewart has hired an Indian named Quamis as his servant. (LT)

April 7

Stephen Bates visits Dr. Seneca Lapham and his assistant Winfield Phillips at Miskatonic University and reveals odd events at the Billington House. (LT)

April 9

A rural mail carrier delivers a fragment of paper addressed to Dr. Lapham and signed by Stephen Bates who is never heard from again. That night Lapham and Winfield Phillips destroy the tower in Billington's Woods and put to rest Ambrose Dewart and Misquamacus. (LT)

April 16

Fred Akeley moves into the Old Wharton Place. (GW)

May

Fred Akeley shatters the glass from Leng and obtains a ". . .cut tentacle ten feet in length . . . no living savant could identify . . .". (GW)

1925

A fisherman is found wandering incoherently after spending a night in a ruined abbey near Manchester. Days later he is found dead in the abbey horribly mangled. (TS)

1927

The Providence Journal publishes a notice concerning the death of Dr. Jean-Francois Charriere who is interred in the garden of his home on Benefit Street, which is held in trust by Baker and Greenbaugh. (SU)

Summer

Fred Hadley of Boston takes refuge from a storm in the farmhouse of Amos Stark. That night though they are miles apart, both Clem Whateley and Amos Stark die. (WD)

1928

Circa

The Charriere House is rented by a professional man and his family but they stay less than a month complaining of dampness and smells. (SU)

James Conrad, his friend Kirowan, and the artist Humphrey Skuyler, and the mayor of Old Dutch Town visit an abandoned farmhouse. The next night Conrad returns and enters the house. A week later Conrad gives Kirowan a phantasmic account of his night in the house. Before Kirowan can intervene Conrad burns the farmhouse down and commits suicide. (HO)

January 17

Wilbur Whateley writes a letter to Septimus Bishop. (HM)

March

Uriah Garrison dies leaving his estate to his great nephew Adam Duncan of Brattleboro, Vermont. (SA)

Before he dies Amos Tuttle reminds his lawyer Mr. Haddon of Boston to follow his will to the letter. After his death his body begins to change dramatically and Dr. Ephraim Sprague orders an immediate entombment in the Tuttle Vault at Arkham Cemetery. Dr. Llanfer is surprised when Haddon returns the Necronomicon to Miskatonic University. Paul Tuttle threatens to challenge the will and consequently the house is not demolished as required. (RH)

April 3

Abel Harrop of Harrop's Pocket is last seen in Aylesbury. (WP)

April 24

Asaph Waite notes that the storm of the previous night had resulted in the sinking of many boats, but none from Innsmouth. (BI)

April 27

A stranger in Innsmouth plies Zadok Allen with liquor. (BI)

Apr 30

Dan Harrop occupies his missing cousin's home in Harrop's Pocket, after which the whippoorwills become frenzied. (WP)

May 3

Lute Corey finds Bert Giles with his throat torn out, two days later seven cows are killed on a local farm. (WP)

May 8

Dan Harrop is arrested for tearing out the throat of Amelia Hutchins while chanting strange words. (WP)

May 21

A Federal man visits the Marsh Refining Company. (BI)

May 23

Rumors about a destroyer in the vicinity of Devil Reef. (BI)

May 27

Strangers in Innsmouth examine the docks. Unfamiliar ships are seen off the coast. (BI)

June

Adam Duncan and his fiancée Rhoda Prentiss move into the house on Aylesbury Street that once belonged to his uncle. Within days Miss Prentiss sets the house ablaze. (SA)

Zadok is dealt with in Innsmouth. (BI)

June 7

Young Horvath Waite of Innsmouth goes to live with relatives in Boston. Sometime after this, but before June 10th, Federal forces in Innsmouth begin blasting the waterfront, and a destroyer is confirmed off Devil Reef. (BI)

June 10

Asaph Waite names Martha and Arnold Blayne of Boston as executors of the trust he creates for his grandson Horvath. (BI)

September

About this time Dr. Llanfer confides in Haddon that the *Necronomicon* has been stolen. (RH)

Fall

Seth Bishop kills Amos Bowden. (HV)

The sculptor Jeffrey Corey returns from Paris and rents a cottage on the coast south of Innsmouth. (IC)

October

The Tuttle Vault in Arkham Cemetery is violated and the coffin of Amos Tuttle is found outside of Arkham. Haddon is summoned to the Tuttle Estate and using explosives planted by Paul Tuttle destroys the house. Something horrible shrieks and gibbers in the flames. (RH)

December

Ken Jack visits his friend sculptor Jeffrey Corey at his cottage south of Innsmouth. (IC)

1929

February

A destroyer is seen dropping depth charges off of Devil Reef. Afterwards a mass of blue clay washes up on the beach which sculptor Jeff Corey gathers up. (IC)

March 6

Sculptor Jeffrey Corey begins documenting his dreams, but does not mention them to his friend Ken Jack who visits not long after. (IC)

March 21

Jeffrey Corey's letter to his friend Ken Jack is his last communication before he disappears. (IC)

April 17

Ken Jack sees something in the waters off Devil Reef that haunts his dreams. (IC)

June

A rash of disappearances culminates with the vanishing of Septimus Bishop, a Harvard educated man about 57 years old. (HM)

Autumn

The last grandson of Asaph Peabody and his wife die in an automobile accident. The Peabody Estate is inherited by their only son who begins restorations. (PH)

October

The artist Jason Phillips and Arnsley, the son of Lord Leveredge, spend a night in a ruined abbey. The next morning Arnsley is found dead in a crypt beneath the abbey and Phillips spends two months in a hospital. (TS)

1930

During a performance of Maugham's *The Letter*, Pr. Amos Piper of Miskatonic University falls into a coma. When he awakens three days later, he has no memory of himself, his sister, Miskatonic University, or Arkham. He also has difficulty with the use of his hands. After less than a month he begins to travel extensively a practice which continues over the next three years. (SS)

February 2

A great grandson of Asaph Peabody occupies restored portions of the Peabody Estate. (PH)

February 25

Allison Wentworth and James MacDonald set out for Stillwater. That night a snowstorm hits and Wentworth, MacDonald and all the residents of Stillwater vanish. (TW)

February 27

The Navissa Daily reports on the Stillwater Mystery. (TW)

March 30

Peter Henrick investigating the Stillwater Mystery finds an abandoned dog sled along with tracks of an unbelievable large thing. (TW)

April 1

The two year old child of George Taylor is taken in the night. (PH)

April 2

Workmen restoring the Peabody Estate uncover something that causes them to abandon their labors. (PH)

Summer?

Alijah Atwood rents the Charriere House on Benefit Street in Providence. His time is cut short after he fires four shots at a bestial thing in the study. (SU)

1931

February 27

Constable Robert Norris submits his report on the Stillwater Mystery. (TW)

March 5

Constable Robert Norris writes of being followed by something with burning eyes. (TW)

March 6

Constable Robert Norris posts his last report. (TW)

March 7

Constable Robert Norris disappears from Navissa Camp. (TW)

Spring

Land reclamation from Lake Michigan in preparation for the Chicago World's Fair dredges up pieces of creatures that Pr. Jordan Holmes of the Field Museum cannot identify. Over the next few days there are many violent deaths including a massacre on the Municipal Pier. Things end after great columns of fire are seen on the lake. (HD)

October 17

The body of Constable Robert Norris is found four miles north of Navissa Camp. (TW)

October 30

In the evening John Dalhousie witnesses three bodies fall out of the sky including those of Allison Wentworth and James MacDonald who are still alive. Wentworth regains consciousness and talks. (TW)

October 31

James MacDonald dies at 10:07 in the morning. Allison Wentworth dies at 3:21 in the afternoon. Dr. Jamison and the Coroner conclude that the cause of death is exposure to warmth. John Dalhousie

Division Chief of the Royal Northwest Mounted Police issues a statement concerning Constable Norris. (TW)

1932

Father Brisbois an itinerant priest twice reports Indian children missing from Cold Harbor. (IT)

1933

Amos Piper recovers from his queer amnesia and is brought to the psychiatrist Dr. Corey for treatment. After almost three weeks he seems to have recovered completely. Ten days later Piper tells Corey he is joining an expedition to the Arabian Desert. Two nights later Corey's office is broken in to and all of Piper's files stolen. Sometime later the entire expedition vanishes. Later still Dr. Nathaniel Corey and an unnamed man are found burning the doctor's papers; they are both confined to the Larkin Institute. (SS)

February 21

In the evening, during a light snowstorm, a neighbor sees Henry Lucas heading for the Olassie Trail. (IT)

February 23

Henry Lucas is reported missing by his brother-in-law Randy Margate. (IT)

February 25

Constable John French arrives in Cold Harbor to investigate the disappearance of John French. Medicine Three Hats tells him that no man may look upon Ithaqua without worship. (IT)

February 27

After meeting with Father Brisbois Constable French spends the afternoon following the Olassie Trail to three stone circles seventy feet in diameter where the snow is smooth like glass. Later that evening he takes refuge at the home of Dr. Telfer and talks with Father Brisbois again. That night Henry Lucas' frozen body is found still alive. He dies three hours later. (IT)

March 3

Constable French finishes writing his report and posts it and then follows Indians into the woods. (IT)

March 4

Dr. Telfer sends a letter saying that Constable French has vanished. (IT)

April

After a lengthy period away Division Chief John Dalhousie finally opens Dr. Telfer's letter. He immediately sends Constable Robert Considine and then within twenty-four hours he himself goes to Cold Harbor where they blow up the stone circles. (IT)

Spring

Newspapers report on the queer beliefs of certain Indian tribes, the vanishing of Henry Lucas, the incompetence of Constable John French, and his subsequent disappearance. (IT)

May 7

During a violent snowstorm the frozen body of Constable John French is found. (IT)

May 11

Division Chief John Dalhousie releases a statement concerning the Lucas Case and Constable John French. Sometime after this Dalhousie goes missing only to be found frozen 3 days later. Afterwards the Canadian government scatters the local tribal members throughout the provinces. (IT)

1934

Abner Whateley inherits the Luther Whateley Home and Mill in Dunwich and knocks down the mill. There follows a series of livestock losses and the death of Luke Lang. Things come to an end when Abner sets fire to the home and drives out of Dunwich like one possessed. (SR)

1935

Circa

The Marsh Family purchase a few ships for their fleet. Ahab Marsh the great grandson of Obed Marsh comes to Innsmouth. (WS)

After being missing for twenty years Pr. Laban Shrewsbury strolls out of his house. (HC)

1936

Jason Warwick's trip to the Lofoten Islands is followed by a series of freezing deaths across the continent and England including the butler of Sir John Hardie. The deaths end after Warwick disappears at Lady Drayton's weekend party. (SM)

Pr. Laban Shrewsbury's monograph on the *R'lyeh Text* is published. (HC)

1937

August 17

The *HMS Advocate* leaves Singapore. (GS)

August 21

The *HMS Advocate* is lost in a storm leaving survivors in lifeboats. (GS)

Fall

With the family fortune dwindling Asa Sandwin leaves Sandwin House and returns some weeks later with the fortune restored. (SC)

December 17

A manuscript purporting to be a record of the fate of the *HMS Advocate* is found in a bottle. (GS)

1938

After stealing an artifact from Salisbury, Phillip Caravel is killed when his London home blows up. (GB)

March

Eldon Sandwin summons his cousin David to Sandwin House to investigate strange events, Asa Sandwin hints at a horrible compact. (SC)

April 27

During a windstorm Asa Sandwin vanishes. (SC)

June

Andrew Phelan, 28, of Boston answers Pr. Laban Shrewsbury of Arkham's ad for an assistant and spends the evening recording an interview with the sailor Timoto Fernandez. The next day Fernandez is reported dead. (HC)

July

A hill collapses into an underground reservoir near Salapunco Peru. (HC)

August 17

The New York Times carries a report on Nayland Massie of London who disappeared seven months earlier only to reappear speaking a language experts cannot identify. (HC)

August 18

Andrew Phelan goes to see the therapist Dr. Asenath DeVoto of Boston. Later he deposits Shrewsbury's papers at the Miskatonic University Library. That night Pr. Laban Shrewsbury is presumed dead when his home collapses and burns. (HC)

September 1

Andrew Phelan vanishes from his Boston Apartment. (HC)

1939

April 3

Eric Holm buys a copy of the *Confessions of the Mad Monk Clithanus* from Sanderton and Harker, Book Importers. He later shows the book to his friend Jeremy Lansing. That night he is pulled to pieces. (PE)

September

Tony Alwyn, an Assistant Librarian at Miskatonic University, travels to Wisconsin to visit his cousin Frolin and grandfather Josiah. Shortly after his arrival Josiah Alwyn vanishes into a cavern over which the house had been built. (BT)

1940

Early

Two stories appear within a week of each other, pilot Joseph X. Castleton sights a large animal bathing in a lake, and the body of Fr. Piregard missing for three centuries is found well preserved inside the trunk of a hollow tree. (DD)

January

Claiborne Boyd begins studying the Creole culture in New Orleans. (GS)

Spring

Pr. Upton Gardner and his secretary Laird Dorgan visit the state museum and are privately shown the body of Fr. Piregard which has begun to quickly decay. (DD)

March

Pr. Asaph Gilman formerly of Harvard and Miskatonic University dies in a Limehouse riot and his papers are inherited by Claiborne Boyd. (GS)

April

Josiah Alwyn's notebook is found in Saskatchewan. (BT)

Summer

Andrew Phelan returns to Boston and with divinity student Abel Keane briefly moves to Arkham. Shortly after, a fire destroys the Marsh Refinery and much of Innsmouth. Abel Keane quits divinity school and begins haunting the Miskatonic University Library until he vanishes. (WS)

July

Claiborne Boyd travels to Lima Peru. (GS)

Pr. Upton Gardner of State University goes to stay at an abandoned cabin on Rick's Lake. (DD)

September

Pr. Upton Gardner goes missing. (DD)

October

Laird Dorgan and Jack go to Rick's Lake shortly before a fire consumes the cabin and surrounding woods. (DD)

November

Claiborne Boyd vanishes near Salapunco Peru. (GS)

The frozen body of Josiah Alwyn is found on an island southeast of Singapore. (BT)

1941

Summer

At the suggestion of his friend Brent Nicholson, the artist Jefferson Bates rents the Bishop House near Aylesbury for the summer. After seven weeks Sereno More and Bud Perkins accuse Bates of killing cows and a mob sets the house ablaze. Bates is arrested for killing Bud Perkins. (HV)

1947

Spring

Pr. Laban Shrewsbury and Nayland Colum, author of *The Watchers on the Other Side*, are lost during a storm on the Red Sea. (KK)

Summer

Within a week Marius Phillips' mother and his uncle Sylvan die and he inherits two homes, one in Innsmouth and one further north on the coast. (SO)

Pinckney gives the art critic Jason Wecter of the Boston Dial an octopoid carving which engenders a dramatic change in his writing that culminates in his disappearance. (SW)

September

During *Operation Ponape*, Laban Shrewsbury, Nayland Colum, Abel Keane, Andrew Phelan, Claiborne Boyd, Horvath Blayne, and Brigadier-General Holberg aboard the destroyer *Hamilton* witness the use of a nuclear weapon. (BI)

November

Marius Phillips and his recent bride Ada Marsh are lost at sea near Ponape. (SO)

1948

Summer

The Reverend Abel Keane drowns while swimming near Gloucester, his body is not recovered. (BI)

Ambrose Bishop reaches Dunwich seven days after leaving London and takes possession of his great uncle Septimus Bishop's farm. Within days Seth Frye and Harold Sawyer vanish leaving Sheriff John Houghton with no leads. Ambrose Bishop vanishes when the Old Bishop House is destroyed by fire. Eleven days later the Old Crary Road Bridge, recently destroyed, is anonymously rebuilt and crowned with an Elder Sign. (HM)

1950

One day Geoffrey Malvern, son of Lord Malvern shows the schoolmaster a star shaped stone and speaks of his intention to visit the ruined Cathedral of Hydestall. That night Constable John Slade of Lynwold brings Geoffrey Malvern who is out of his head to Doctor William Currie. There follows a series of strange events and deaths which only ended after Currie and some of Malvern's friends return to Hydestall. (ST)

1953

Dr. Ambrose Perry retires to a home near Tyburn Vermont to pursue unorthodox research. (TA)

1956

Dr. Ambrose Perry is killed by his own dog about a month after his cousin Henry comes to visit. (TA)

1965

Early July

Arthur Phillips confesses to setting fire to a house along the Seekonk in Providence after rescuing Rose Dexter from it. Inside the police find charred flesh that is not human. About a week later on the Sixteenth, Rose Dexter kills Arthur Phillips after he attacks her. (DB)

MORE BOOKS FROM LOVECRAFT EZINE PRESS
(available at Amazon):

The King in Yellow Tales volume I, by Joseph S. Pulver, Sr.

The Sea of Ash, by Scott Thomas

READ THE LOVECRAFT EZINE:

www.lovecraftzine.com

www.ingramcontent.com/pod-product-compliance
Lightning Source LLC
Chambersburg PA
CBHW022135280326
41933CB00007B/702